CAMPOBELLO

LECTOR HOUSE PUBLIC DOMAIN WORKS

CAMPOBELLO

KATE GANNETT WELLS

ISBN: 978-93-5614-599-3

Published: -

LECTOR HOUSE LLP
E-MAIL: info@lectorhouse.com

CAMPOBELLO
AN HISTORICAL SKETCH

BY

KATE GANNETT WELLS

For those who are desirous of exact knowledge concerning thep "Story of the Boundary Line," and the political history of Eastport and its vicinity, there is no more comprehensive work than that by William Henry Kilby, Esq., entitled, "Eastport and Passamaquoddy." To him, and also to two friends who kindly gave me the names of a few of the Island flowers, do I express my gratitude.

CAMPOBELLO.

THE mysterious charms of ancestry and yellow parchment, of petitions to the admiralty and royal grants of land, of wild scenery and feudal loyalty, of rough living and knightly etiquette, have long clustered round a little island off the coast of Maine, called on the charts Passamaquoddy Outer Island, but better known under the more pleasing name of Campobello.

Its Discovery. It belongs to the region first discovered by the French, who, under Sieur De Monts, in the spring of 1604, sailed along the shores of Nova Scotia, and gave the name of Isle of Margos (magpies) to the four perilous islands now called The Wolves; beheld Manthane (now Grand Manan); sailed up the St. Croix; and established themselves on one of its islands, which they called the Isle of St. Croix. The severity of the winter drove them in the following summer to Annapolis, and for more than a hundred and fifty years little was known of this part of the country, though the River St. Croix first formed the boundary between Acadia and New England, and later the boundary between the Provinces of Nova Scotia and Massachusetts Bay.

Campobello itself could scarcely be said to have a history till towards the end of the eighteenth century. Moose roamed over the swamps and looked down from the bold headlands; Indians crossed from the mainland and shot them; straggling Frenchmen, dressing in skins, built huts along the northern and southern shores, till civilization dawned through the squatter sovereignty of two men, Hunt and Flagg. They planted the apple trees whose gnarled branches still remain to tell of the winter storms that howled across the plains, and converted the moose-yards into a field of oats, for the wary, frightened animals vacated their hereditary land in favor of these usurpers. Their mercantile skill taught them how to use, for purposes of trade rather than for private consumption, the shoals of fish which it was firmly believed Providence sent into the bay.

Post Office. There were not enough inhabitants to justify the maintenance of a post office till 1795; then the mails came once in two weeks. Lewis Frederic Delesdernier was the resonant, high sounding name of the first postmaster who lived at Flagg's Point (the Narrows). But when a post office was opened in Eastport, in 1805, this little Island one was abandoned, or rather it dwindled out of existence before the larger one established by Admiral Owen at Welsh Pool.

Welsh Pool. The Narrows, because of its close proximity to the mainland, was a favorite place of abode in those early days. Yet Friar's Bay, two miles to the north, was a safe place for boats in easterly storms; and thus, before the advent of the Owens, a hamlet had clustered around what is now called Welsh Pool. A Mr. Curry was the pioneer. The house opposite the upper entrance to the Owen domain was called Curry House until it became "the parsonage," a name abandoned when the present rectory was built. Curry traded with the West Indies, and owned, it is said, two brigs and a bark.

People also gathered at the upper end of the Island, Wilson's Beach, and on the road between Sarawac and Conroy's Bridge, where there were several log houses.

Garrison's Grandparents. That some kind of a magistrate or minister even then was on the Island is attested by the fact that William Lloyd Garrison's grandparents, Andrew Lloyd and Mary Lawless, chanced to come to Nova Scotia on the same ship from Ireland, and were married to each other "the day after they had landed at Campobello, March 30, 1771." Lloyd became a commissioned pilot at Quoddy, and died in 1813. His wife was the first person buried in Deer Island. Their daughter Fanny was Garrison's mother.

Many of the early inhabitants were Tories from New York. Some were of Scotch origin, especially those who lived on the North Road.

Captain Storrow. Among these settlers was a young British officer, Captain Thomas Storrow, who, while he was prisoner of war, fell in love with Ann Appleton, a young girl of Portsmouth, N.H. In vain did her family object, "British officers being less popular then than now; but young love prevailed," and the marriage, which took place in 1777, "was a happy one." Captain Storrow took his bride to England; but after a while sailed for Halifax, where they remained "nearly two years." In 1785 they went to St. Andrews. Through the courtesy of their grandson, Colonel Thomas Wentworth Higginson, the following extract is given from a manuscript sketch of the life of Mrs. Storrow, prepared by her niece, Mrs. Norman Williams:—

False Sale. "Soon after this (1785) they removed to Campobello, which had been purchased by Mr. Butler and Captain Storrow. There were two houses on the Island, one for each family, and here they lived very happily and pleasantly. There was always a garrison at St. Andrews, and a ship of war stationed near Campobello; so Captain Storrow had congenial society, and they had many pleasant lady friends, and, as their hospitality was unbounded, they were seldom without company at one or the other of the houses.... All was bright and prosperous. But a change came. In 1790 or 1791 the Butlers and Captain Storrow had gone to Halifax on business, and Mrs. Storrow was left alone with her children on the Island, when a notice was served to her that she must quit the Island immediately, as it had been sold to them under a false title, and the real owner had come to take possession. The Island had been granted by William Pitt to his former tutor, David Owen, a hard man who would not move from the position he had taken. Mrs. Storrow sent to my father, who was her husband's lawyer, and he, with some other gentlemen, chartered a sloop and brought the family to St. Andrews, where a house was already prepared for them. Here they remained a year or more. But Capt. Storrow's finances were so crippled by the loss of Campobello that he and his family sailed for Jamaica, where he had a small estate."

William Owen. David Owen, to whom this manuscript referred, was a cousin of William Owen, through whom the Island became connected by royal gift and by romance with the fortunes of his immediate descendants. As naval officer William Owen had been "in all the service and enterprise where ships, boats, and seamen were employed," had labored at Bengal for the re-establishment of the affairs of the East India Company, and had fought under Clive. At the blockade of Pondicherry he lost his right arm, and the Sunderland, to which he belonged, having foundered, he was ordered to England. Broken in spirit and weak in body, the copy of what was presumably his memorial to the Admiralty in 1761 has a piteous sound. It begins:—

His Petition. "My Lord, permit me, with the most profound respect, to lay by your Lordship a true State of my past service, with the accidents that happened to me during the same, praying your Lordship not to judge hard of me, in being reduced to the disagreeable necessity of doing that myself which would appear in a much more favorable light were any of my Friends in Town who could take the Liberty of Introducing me to your Lordship." After recounting the services he rendered, and the injuries he received, he ends with these words: "I beg you will be pleased to represent to the Right Honorable the Lords of the Admiralty that I am the person mentioned in Admiral Steuen's [the spelling is illegible] Letter to have lost my Right Arm, when I had the Honor of Commanding one of the Divisions of Boats ordered by him to cut out the Two French Ships, La Baline and Hermione, from under the Guns of Pondicherry, on the 7th of October last, and that I had been wounded before in that country with a Musket Ball, which lodged in my Body above three years and a half. My long service in the East Indies, together with the Wounds I received, having greatly impaired my health, lays me under a necessity to be the more urgent with you on this occasion, that I may the sooner go into the Country to endeavor to re-establish the same, as well as to see my Friends, from whom I have been above nine years absent. Let me, therefore, Sir, entreat you to move their Lordships in my behalf, humbly praying that they will be pleased to direct something to be done for me, either by Gratuity, Pension, or Preferment, such as their Lordships may deem me to deserve."

Sir William Campbell. In November of the same year he writes to Lord William Campbell: "I arrived in London above four months ago. After long attendance and great solicitations, I am at length put off with a pitiful Pension, with which I am going to retire into the Country among my Relations for the remainder of my days, unless somewhat unexpected happens to enable me to obtain the promotion I think I have a right to.... I have spent a great deal of money in Town, have no Fortune, and want a sum soon on a very urgent Occasion.... I hope, notwithstanding the disparity between us in point of Rank and Fortune, that your Lordship will honor me with a Continuance of the Friendship and Regard which I had reason to imagine subsisted between us during the five years we Messed together."

This beseeching letter must have been effectual; for in course of time he did receive, not only thanks and promise of promotion, but through the intercession of his friend, Sir William Campbell, who was Governor General of Nova Scotia, he obtained possession of the Island which Hunt and Flagg had ruled.

Royal Grant. As it embraced more land than could then be granted to one person, Owen induced others to join him in asking for the grant, that the whole Island might eventually be under control of the Owen family.

Origin of Name. Consequently, in 1767, the Island was deeded to William Owen and his cousins, Arthur Davies, David and William Owen, Jr., who, in grateful compliment to Campbell, changed its name from Passamaquoddy Outer Island to Campobello, thus "punning on the donor's name, and also expressing the beauty of the natural scenery." It was like the Admiral to invent a name which should include both a joke and a subtle allusion to his classical learning.

First Colony. William Owen immediately brought over from the mother country a colony of seventy persons; stationed his ship at Havre De Lute, a Franco-Indian corruption of Harbor of the Otter; and, having settled his people according to his liking, returned to England; but soon left it again on public service, and died with the rank of Admiral.

David Owen. David Owen acted as agent for the grantees, and was a veritable lord of the Island, always interested in protecting the fisheries. His house, near the site of the cottage now owned by James Roosevelt, Esq., had even more roof than the usual sloping, barn-like home of former days. He built a rude church, read the service, and preached. What matter if the sermon was oft repeated, or now and then was original! Could not he, though a layman, best tell the needs of his congregation? He played the fiddle for dances, married the people, scolded them as a self-constituted judge, and kept a journal of Island events in microscopic chirography. He was an occasional correspondent of the "Eastport Sentinel" on matters of British history and theological controversy. "He had a fine library of old books, and was well versed in scholastic subjects," said Dr. Andrew Bigelow, the first Unitarian minister of Eastport, who often visited him.

To "Hue and Cry." Once David Owen committed to the gaol in St. Andrews a Frenchman, for "feloniously taking and carrying away some fish from flakes at Campobello." As the offender went on his way to gaol in his own vessel, he threw overboard the deputy sheriff who accompanied him, drew his dirk on the other man and compelled him to follow, and then escaped himself with his own vessel. Therefore, Owen advertised in the "Sentinel" of September 25, 1819, "To all officers and others to whom the execution hereof may belong ... to search for the said Appleby [the Frenchman], and therefore to '*hue* and *cry*' after him as the law directs." Signed "D. Owen, J.P."

When David died he left his share of the land to William Owen, Jr. This younger Owen sold Campobello, which had now come into his sole possession, to William Fitz-William, who, as the natural son of the Owen of Pondicherry fame, could obtain possession only through purchase of his father's grant.

Primitive Life. Island life was still very primitive. The people raised stock, and the creatures fed on the wild grass and young hemlock. But, as David had freely deeded the land to the settlers, the underbrush was soon killed off and stock raising ceased. The Campobellians also proved no exception to the rule that agriculture is seldom a favorite occupation with those who can support themselves by the precarious life of fishermen, even if that has its perils.

Illness. Here, too, as everywhere in pioneer life, the women suffered as much as, if not more than, the men. When sickness came upon them they endured it patiently, with that kind of meek despair which looks upon illness either as fate or as the will of the Lord. Fortunately for them, a young girl, who had been born on the Island, became at sixteen a skilful nurse. She was sought from far and near, and taken out at night when she had to be blindfolded on account of the storms. The description of one of her visits must be given in her own words, as she told it when she was eighty-four:—

The Indian's Squaw. "Once I and my husband were abed a howling night, and I heard a knock. Says I, 'Jim, I bet that's for me; get up and see.' And I sorter guessed it was a foreigner. And he came back and says, 'P. (that's what he called me, short for Parker), it's an Indian from down on the Narrows; and he's been for the doctor, and he's down at Robinson, and won't be fetched 'cause he's having a good time.' So I got up and dressed and went down with him; for the squaw's skin was as dear to her husband as a white woman's is to her, and her heart may be just as good to God. And when I got there I saw two squaws, and one was all in a heap; and they made eyes at me, and I didn't know whether it meant murder or not, only I guessed not. And I says, 'Sister, what is it?' And she says, her husband tell her 'white doctor no come. You white woman come and make his squaw live.' So I went to work. And when all was right, they wanted me to take a blanket and lie down; but I could no way make believe Indian, so I sits up till morning. Then the Indian asked me what he should give me; and I told him my gineral price was three dollars, but when folks was no better off than I, I turned in and asked nothin'. And he says, 'We give five dollars if it's a girl, and three dollars if it's a boy.' 'Well,' I says, 'sure enough it's a boy'; and I come home. And next day he travels down here [to the Pool], and says me better than man doctor, and wished he could give me twenty dollars."

Some sixty years after this incident had occurred, when Mrs. Parker was driven up to the Narrows where the squaw had lived, and past the Tyn-Y-Coed and cottages, that she might see the changes which time had wrought, she exclaimed, "As the Bible says, now I can die in peace, for mine eyes have seen the salvation, I will not say of the Lord, but of Campobello."

The Admiral. The salvation, such as it was, came slowly; at first through Admiral William Fitz-William Owen. His life was curious and pathetic, from the time when a boy five years old, an inmate of the artillery barracks, he replied, on being asked his last name, "I don't know, mother can tell you," to his old age, when, dressed in admiral's uniform, he paced back and forth on a plank walk, built out into the bay, over the high cliffs of the shore, in memory of the quarter deck of his beloved ship. Conceited and religious, authoritative and generous, humorous and ceremonious, disputatious and frank, a lover of women more than of wine, his fame still lingers in many a name and tradition.

His Growth. When very young, a friend of his father's took him away from the barracks and from his mother, of whom he never again heard. He was boarded and punished in various homes in North Wales, but as recompense wore a cocked hat and a suit of scarlet made from an old coat of his father, —"the first sensible mark of the earthly pre-existence of some one who claimed to be my father" he had ever received, wrote the Admiral, in his later days. He learned the catechism and collects, repeated the Lord's prayer on his knees, and thought of raising the devil by saying it backwards; but he never completed the charm, and for four or five years after was self-punished by his fear that the devil was waiting for him at the church door.

By degrees he learned something of his father, the William Owen of Pondicherry fame, who had died while he was a baby. When about fourteen he went to a mathematical academy, where his "progress was as remarkable as it had before been in classics." Here religious instruction consisted in going to church "to talk with our fingers to the girls of a school who used the adjoining pew." As a boy, he "had no other distinct idea of our Lord Jesus Christ than that he was a good man."

His Dreams. His belief in the direct interposition of the Creator on his behalf frequently solaced him in these youthful days of loneliness and misdemeanor. The literal and instant fulfillment of two dreams on special and unthought-of subjects were convincing proof, to quote his own words, that "they were sent by God Almighty himself, as a simple way of assuring me that as I was under his eye he would himself take care of me."

Man-of-War Garden. So he grew up to be presumptuous, adventurous, resolute, and strong. In 1788 he became a midshipman in a line-of-battle ship, in due course of time cruising in the Bay of Fundy. For three years his man-of-war was stationed at Campobello. The crew often went ashore in summer, tending a little garden at Havre de Lutre (Harbor of the Otter), called Man-of-War Garden, which in turn gave its name to the headland. The garden was brilliant with dahlias and marigolds, which were presented in overweighted bouquets to the few Island belles, who, in return for such unexpected courtesies, consented in winter to dance on the ship's deck, regardless of their frozen ear-tips. Two of the midshipmen were as dauntless in pedestrianism as in love, and for a wager started on a perilous walk around icy cliffs which threw them headlong. Their comrades buried them under the gay flowers, and sailed away from the henceforth ill-omened garden. And the little store near by, kept by one Butler, lost its customers and passed into tradition.

The Boy as Midshipman. With Owen's entrance into the naval service as boy officer "commenced," he wrote in later years, "a public life which may be said to have had no sensible intermission until the close of 1831, or forty-three years; during which I have served under every naval man of renown, and was honored by the friendship of Nelson. From the year 1797 I have held commands and been entrusted with some important service, for the most part in remote parts of the world. My character, if I may be allowed to draw it myself, contained much of good and bad. The latter, perhaps, I contrived to veil sufficiently not to mar my reputation; but, by the grace of God, he has not left me without his spirit of self-conviction.... At forty-four I married [a Miss Evans, of Welsh extraction]. I thought myself a tolerably religious man, but knew myself to be as Reuben, unstable as water. At fifty-seven my worldly ambition was barred by corruption in high places. At sixty-one I became the 'Hermit.'"

His Settlement at Campobello. "The Quoddy Hermit," — this was the name he chose when, with the rank of admiral, he came back to Campobello to live. He brought with him building material and the frame of a house taken from Rice's Island, and erected his habitation where is now the Owen. In the grove at the northern end of the present hotel he planted two or three English oaks. He placed the sun dial of his vessel in the garden fronting his house, and put a section of his beloved quarter deck close to the shore, not far from the seedling oaks. There, pacing up and down in uniform, he lived over again the days of his attack upon the Spanish pirate. Proud as he was of the two cannon he then captured, there is no one living to tell who bled or who swore, or whether the Spanish galleon sank or paid ransom. He placed the cannon on the Point, where they bid defiance to American fishing boats. In later years one was taken to Flagstaff Hill whenever a salute was to be given in honor of the Queen's birthday, or a fish fair, for such fairs were famous.

Weddings. The population of the Island increased, and the old man married the boys and girls at church or at home, slowly or hastily, as his humor bade him, always claiming the first kiss of the bride. A certain sailor who had wooed a Campobello maiden was determined that this privilege should not be allowed by her, and therefore tried to salute his bride before the service was ended. "You are not married yet. Back!" shouted the Admiral. Frightened, the sailor-groom turned his face and his feet toward the minister-magistrate, who more and more slowly repeated the words of the service, as he approached nearer to the lady, till, with the last word, he snatched the first kiss. His most princely gift as a wedding present is said to have been the Island of Pope's Folly, a present conditioned on his performance of the marriage service, which was gladly granted by the bride.

He widened the narrow roads along the bay, which David had broken out, and in his heavy, lumbering coach of state went through snow and mud from one tenant to another. The coach is still to be seen, and the tenants' grandchildren bear the Owen surname as the universal Christian cognomen. The Admiral would often stroll down to Whale-Boat Cove, — so called from a large kind of row-boat used in the herring fisheries, — which he persuaded the men to call Welsh Pool. Many a little maiden counted her pennies by the Admiral's kisses, and many a poor fisherman blessed him for allowing the house rent to run on from year to year, though the Admiral invariably insisted on the rental from the weirs; he well knew which was the more profitable.

Family Life. On other days he stayed at home and amused himself with his books. At four o'clock the husband and wife dined with the family and the frequent guests. The dinner of four courses was served in silver and gold lined dishes, with wines from Jersey and game from the Provinces. Silver candelabras shone upon the table; damask and India muslin curtains shaded the many paned windows; heavy mahogany and rosewood chairs, sofas, and tables furnished the apartments; great logs on tall andirons burned in monster fireplaces; sacred maps hung around the evening parlor; and the dining-room carpet was said to have been a gift from the King of Prussia. The long curved mahogany sofa, the carved chairs, and other pieces of furniture are now owned by the Islanders. The library table and arm chair, with sockets in its arms for candles, the Admiral's hat, pistols, and picture are carefully treasured by "The Company" as relics.

After the dinner of an hour came tea at seven and a family rubber till nine; then Scripture reading and worship, when the ladies and servants retired, leaving the Admiral and his gentlemen friends, fortified with cigars, whiskey, and water, to relate naval stories and discuss religious themes till two or three o'clock in the morning.

Theology. Owen's three chosen intimates were designated Academicus, Rusticus, and Theophilus. His library, which they frequently consulted, was a sad medley of dictionaries and the theology of Oxford divines. Methodism and Romanism were alike hateful to the hermit Admiral, who, in quoting from Holy Writ, always rendered "the wiles" as "the methodisms" of the devil. Every week he read to his neighbors two lectures "from unexceptionable sources, yet so modified as to contain all that was expedient to explain of his peculiar opinions." Often he held church service in what was almost a shanty, omitting from the liturgy whatsoever he might chance to dislike on any special Sunday.

Family Prayers. The day began and ended with prayers, which all the household servants attended, the "maids," as the Admiral called them, —"for we are all servants of God," —bringing their work and sewing throughout the service, except when the prayer itself was said. If some one occasionally was disinclined to such steady improvement of the devotional hour, the Admiral, with a benevolent smile, inquired, "My dear, do you feel lazy to-night?"

Breakfast was served at nine. After that, the Lady Owen, clad in an enormous apron, entered the kitchen and taught the mysteries of salads and jellies.

Lady Owen. Lady Owen was queen as he was king; and never did a lady rule more gently over store-room and parlor, over Sunday-School and sewing-school, fitting the dresses of her domestics or of the Island children. She was a handsome woman, with silver hair and pink and white complexion, who, like her daughters, wore long trains and low corsages. Sometimes the mother wrapped herself in a certain gold and black scarf with such a courtly grace that its remembrance has never faded. Great was the jubilee among the domestics when a box arrived from England, with fabulous dresses ready made.

Once a year the maids and men of the great house had a ball, the ladies playing for them even all night. Twice in the twelve months occurred house-cleaning, when a dress was given each busy worker. The servants were often reminded to take no more than was necessary on their plates; for economy, though not parsimony, was the rule of the house. Guests came from the mainland and from every vessel of war. Admiral Owen and his house were the fashion for many long years.

Nowhere on the coast of Maine has there been a more curious mingling of rank, with its investiture of ceremony, and of simple folk-life, of loyalty to the Queen and her representatives and of the American spirit of personal independence.

Theatricals. All the people were familiar with the great family, while the better part of them were bidden to theatrical performances, for which the Admiral composed songs. It is doubtful whether he chose as early hours for his amateur shows as did the theatre manager of New Brunswick; for on the first occasion of a dramatic performance in that Province, March 28, 1789, the doors were opened at half-past five and the play began at half-past six o'clock.

Other merry-makings occurred on the Island, justified, perhaps, by the occasional homage of gifts sent to the mother country; for the Admiral's diary bears record that "three large, eleven middle, and fourteen small, masts were hoisted on board a vessel, and sent as a tribute to England." Then, whenever a roof-raising occurred, he knew how to send the children home to look after the chores, that their elders might join in the merriment.

Smugglers' Cave. The inhabitants themselves were rather enterprising in business; for rum and lumber were exchangeable quantities with the venturesome Campobello captains, who traded with the southern ports and West Indies, and carried Nova Scotia grindstones to the States. Bolder, but the quieter in action, were the smugglers, who, deep amid the woods, near the only fresh-water pond of the Island, alternately came and vanished. Much of their spare time was spent in digging for an iron chest of Spanish doubloons, buried by ancient buccaneers. The Admiral and his family often rode through the woods to watch the men in their hopeless work, and to obtain their share of treasure-trove if ever it were found. One bright morning every digger had fled, leaving a deep excavation in the ground; but far down on its side, marked out by the iron rust which had clung to the earth, the outlines of a chest were visible. A cart track and the ruins of four or five huts are all that now remain of the site of this mysterious activity. With the departure of these smugglers disappeared the steady excitement of years, the perpetual topic of conversation. Thereafter the people could only question each other about the strange wreck whose rotting timbers were old a century before. Its last remnants have now been carved into love tokens.

Saddest were the days when the Admiral strode up and down his imaginary quarter-deck, his empire a fishing settlement, where boys' wages had once been three cents a day. Eastport still owned the islands around it. The people brought in their fish, and sold it for groceries and other articles at stores where it was credited to them. The little vessels crossing the bay made it gay for the Admiral's eyes. But his spirit sank, as he fancied that some boat might be drifting around an inlet, with its owner frozen to the mast amid the supplies he was bringing to his family, who were waiting in vain for the father to return; or as he thought of the burden of this ever-increasing debit and credit system, or of the perils of the smugglers.

Later, when the duties were taken off by the United States, smuggling disappeared, and Campobello business went down. Could it ever have been said to exist? A few persons possessed enough ready money to build the picturesque weirs which fringe the Island with their stakes, driven three or four feet apart, and ribboned together with small round poles. The dried foliage and the dripping seaweed clinging to them give a ghastly beauty to this living mausoleum of the herring.

The Bank. Remittances did not always come promptly from England, and money was needed in the Island; so the Admiral set up his own bank, and issued one-dollar certificates, surmounted by the crest and his motto, "Flecti non Frangi." But somehow the time never came when he was called upon "to pay one dollar on demand to the bearer at Welsh Pool," and the certificates remain, to be utilized, perhaps, under a new epoch of good will and foolish trust.

Titles. The Island must have had some law and order before the advent of the Admiral, for the town records for the parish of Campobello date from April 15, 1824, James M. Parker, town clerk. At the general session of the peace, holden at St. Andrews, the shire town of Charlotte County, New Brunswick, thirty-two officers were chosen for the small population of Campobello. As in the old German principalities, every Welsh Pooler must have craved a title. There were commissioners and surveyors of highways, overseers of poor and of fisheries, assessors, trustees of schools, inspectors of fish for home consumption and for exports, for smoked herring and boxes. There were cullers of staves, fence-viewers and hog-reeves, and surveyors of lumber and cordwood, lest that which should properly be used for purposes of building or export be consumed on andirons or in kitchen stoves.

Paupers. In those days there was no poorhouse; though town paupers existed, for one, Peter Lion by name, was boarded about for one hundred dollars, and furnished with suitable food, raiment, lodging, and medical aid. No one kept him long at a time, whether it was because others wanted the price paid for his support, or because he was an unwelcome inmate, is unknown. Prices depend on supply; therefore, it happened that the next pauper was boarded for fifty dollars. Again, a lower price for board brought about a lower tax rate for the householders; and, in course of time, another pauper was set up at public auction, and the lowest bidder was entrusted with his care and maintenance.

By 1829 the exports from the Island justified the creation of harbor masters and port wardens,—more titles to be coveted.

Ferryman. A ferry was established from Campobello to Indian Island and Eastport. The ferryman was "recognized in the sum of two pounds, and was conditioned to keep a good and sufficient boat, with sails and oars, to carry all persons who required between the appointed places, to ask, demand, and receive for each person so ferried one shilling and three pence, and no more." If any other than the appointee should have the hardihood to make a little money by transporting a weary traveller, such persons should be fined ten shillings, half of it to go to the informer and half to the ferryman, unless he had previously arranged with the licensee that he would afford him due and righteous satisfaction for each person so carried.

As the population grew, the swine began to abound, and soon it was decreed that "neither swine nor boar-pig should go at large, unless sufficiently ringed and yoked, sucking pigs excepted, on pain of five shillings for each beast."

Sheep. Then the sheep began to jump fences four feet high,—and their descendants have increased in agility. They ate the young cabbages, and standing at ease, defiantly and lazily nipped off the dahlia buds. The town bestirred itself. Angry housewives, roused from their sleep by waking dreams of depredations committed, drove the sheep away with stock and stone. The following night the fisher-husbands, back from their business, sallied forth in vain; they could not run as fast as the women. And week after week the sheep took all they wanted. It became necessary finally to establish the sublime order of hog-reeves, who were privileged to seize any swine or sheep going at large which were not marked with the proper and duly entered mark of the owner, and to prosecute as the law directs; all cattle being ordered to be at home by eight o'clock in the evening. But how could sheep be marked when their fleece forbade their being branded? As notable housekeepers vie with each other in receipts, so did each Islander try to invent striking deformities for his sheep; only the sucking lambs retained their birthrights till their later days. Because Mulholland made two slits in the right ear and took off its top, Parker cut off a piece from the left ear of his sheep, and Bowers made a crop under the left ear of his animal, close to its head. Yet the sheep ran loose until the people were directed to raise twelve pounds for building two cattle pounds, and William Fitz-William Owen, the Admiral, was appointed to erect the same.

The poor rates had again lessened,—woe to the pauper boarder,—for the Admiral wanted money for many another improvement on which his mind was bent. The General Sessions of the peace dared not neglect any suggestion which was made by a man who entertained all the distinguished guests who came to Passamaquoddy Bay; for his fame had spread far and wide as host, theologian, and magnate.

Geese. If it were difficult to restrain sheep and swine, still more difficult was it to prevent the trespasses of geese; though many a bird was clipped in its infancy, and in winter killed and put down amid layers of snow, and sent to the Admiral as a peace offering or as tribute.

Still the public troubles increased; until it was ordered that horses and cattle should be impounded. Then peace by midnight and safety by day rested over the Island. For it was even resolved "that all dogs of six months old and upward should be considered of sufficient age to pay the tax"; but in what manner they were compelled to offer their own excuse for being remains unsolved. Perhaps no legal quibble was ever raised concerning the wording of the statute.

Bridges. Admiral Owen was not only the magistrate for animals, but a builder of bridges, letting out the work "at the rate of $1.12½ per man per day, the day being ten hours of good and conscientious work for man or yoke of oxen."

Nomination Day. Very graphic is an account of "Nomination Day," given by Mr. William H. Kirby, in the "Eastport Sentinel" of June 10, 1885. On the results of this day depended honors and duties. "Four members are to be chosen. Among those put in nomination is the Honorable Captain William Fitz-William Owen, of Campobello, representative of the Island and champion of the fisheries.

A poll being demanded, the real contest is postponed to a later day; starting at St. Andrews, and proceeding from parish to parish, gathering the votes of each neighborhood, until at the end of a fortnight Indian Island is reached, and the voters of West Isles and Campobello have their turn. This affords a good opportunity for curious Eastporters to look in upon the time-honored election processes of the British Empire.

The surroundings of the hustings are rude and characteristic. On a platform made by spreading a plank on the top of fish hogsheads the sheriff of the county has established himself, with his clerks, the candidates and their representatives ranged along. As this is Captain Owen's own precinct, special efforts have been made to bring up his vote, which has somewhat lagged in other parishes; some of the free and independent electors, arriving by the numerous boats which line the beach, wear badges with the motto, "Owen Roads and Bridges," and there are signs that open houses are kept somewhere in the neighborhood. With staunch friends, the Captain has bitter opponents. For the purpose of increasing the income from his Island, he had not long before established a system of pasturage which included a small annual sum for geese, and it is said that at St. Andrews the other day a goose was borne aloft in derision of his candidacy.

Each candidate having urged his claims in an address, the polls are opened and the voting begins. As the elector comes forward, he is asked for whom he votes. The reply is, "Captain Owen," — "Thank you, sir," from Captain Owen; and the same from Mr. Hill, Mr. Brown, Mr. Boyd, Mr. Clinch, or some other candidate, in response to a vote for either. And the clerk enters the several votes upon his record. Each elector can vote for four candidates. Sometimes he names but one; this is a plumper, and elicits cheers. Sometimes a man is asked on what he votes, and replies "Freehold by heir," or something else. I believe that under certain conditions a man could vote in half a dozen counties if he had property.

Closing here, the sheriff, candidates, and special friends adjourn to St. Andrews for the final proceedings. Numbers of votes have been withheld for effective use in the final struggle. Some of the candidates are already so far ahead that their success is assured, and others are hopelessly behind, while for one or more places two or three candidates are separated by only narrow margins, and this affords opportunity for trades and combinations which add zest to the last spasmodic efforts. Captain Owen was not successful this time, though he was chosen at a later campaign, and was afterwards promoted to a seat in Her Majesty's Council for the Province."

Wilson's Claim. The Admiral's life was embittered by the obstinacy with which some of the people refused to pay him allegiance. They were the descendants of one Wilson, who, in David's time, had squatted at Head Harbor, and had built across the end of the Island a bush fence, which was considered to give the sanctity of a written deed to Wilson's claim. David Owen contested the validity of custom, and a lawsuit followed, which was decided in favor of the squatter. This decision was very embarrassing to David, who feared that through its effect he might lose possession of another neck of land. So he hastened home from the court, outstripping his rival, and told a squatter who lived on a second point of the

Island that, as the verdict in the Head Harbor case had been rendered in the Owen favor, he had better sell out at once, or else the law would make him do so. This reasoning, though illogical, was convincing; and the terrified fisherman is reported to have made a lawful deed of his possessions to David for a round of pork, an old gun, and two or three other articles. When Wilson arrived, belated by the wind and tide, the fraud or joke was discovered; but, as no remedy was found for it, the Owens ruled all the Island, except the peninsula which David and his coheirs and successors always called "Wilson's Encroachment." There Wilson and his followers established a thriving settlement, whose prosperity was a constant grievance to the Admiral when he came to live at Campobello. Neither flattery or bribery could induce them to become his vassals. Years after, in the American Civil War, when Captain Robinson, the Admiral's son-in-law, demanded that rents should be paid in English money, Campobello was impoverished, while the people at Wilson's Beach had no rent to pay.

The Cannon. The cannon still remained as sentinels, till some one on board the brig Sam French, which was going to California for gold, stole them and carried them round Cape Horn. When the brig reached San Francisco it fired a salute; but as the Admiral had forewarned the Southern authorities of the capture of his guns, the timely or untimely salute betrayed their presence, and the guns were seized and returned to Campobello. After the removal of the Owen family to England, one of the guns, which had been bought from them by Mr. Best, an Island resident at that time, was given by him to General Cleaves, who placed it on one of the islands in Portland harbor, where two or three years ago it exploded and was shattered to pieces. The other gun was bought by George Batson, Esq., and was placed in his store on the Island, where it became an object of wonder to all newcomers.

Schools. The official dignities of the Admiral increased with his longer residence on Campobello. He was overseer of the poor, postmaster, and school trustee. For a long period there were only private schools; but about fifty years ago the first public or parish school was built near the Taylor House, now Hotel Byron. Four other schools were established at various points; one at Curry's Cove, or Sarawac, — so named by Admiral Owen after a fishing hamlet in Wales, — where Lady Owen and her daughters maintained a vigorous Sunday School.

The Mail. The mails, which were brought by vessel from St. Andrews, came twice a week in summer, and once a week in winter; though it was no uncommon event to wait three weeks for a letter, if the weather were stormy. The people from Indian and Deer Islands came to the Admiral's to get their letters; but woe to any one who chanced to arrive too early in the morning, before the noble postmaster had finished his breakfast.

Survey Book. A curious manuscript book with parchment covers is still extant, labelled on one side, "Register Book, Deeds, Leases, etc., for the estate of Campobello. The property of Captain W. F. W. Owen, R. N. June, 1835." On the other side is written, "Survey Book." It contains several early survey maps of the National Boundary, of the Narrows at Campobello, and of Casco Bay. There are also leases of smoke-houses and weirs. The latter then rented for fifty or sixty dollars a year, and a system of ground-rent prevailed. The Admiral could not have anticipated much income from his possessions; for he speaks of the people as "fishermen, about four hundred in number, very few of whom are, I fear, able to please turn over to pay rent otherwise than in produce,—that is, dried fish and potatoes."

Tyn-Y-Coed. In this same record book he writes that the farm called Tyn-Y-Coed, or The House in the Woods, is so named from "the estate in Montgomery shire, late of Owen Owen, Esq., and Sir Arthur Davies Owen, his son, and William Owen, the youngest son, let to John Gregg, for ten years on his life, at the rate of (6½ s.) six shillings and sixpence." On the oldest map owned by the present Company, drawn by one John Wilkinson, in 1830, the Tyn-Y-Coed and also Lake Glen Severn are designated. The land opposite the Tyn-Y-Coed, where now is the Wells Cottage, used to be called Mount Pleasant.

The Admiral's domains extended beyond Campobello to Head Harbor, Pope's Folly, Sandy, Spruce, and Casco Islands. Since his reign some of these islands have been sold, while Casco Island was given to Chief Justice Allen, of New Brunswick, by Lady Owen. When the little fishing vessels and ferry boats, which ply between these islands, and the big schooners and large steamers, are now counted on any one summer day, it is difficult to realize how comparatively uncrossed were these waters in the Admiral's early years of Island life.

First Steamboat. The first steamboat in New Brunswick was not launched till April, 1816, and then it went only as far as Portland; and a second steamer was not added till 1825. The first New Brunswick newspaper fortunately was issued in 1783, so that it must have been able to announce this new maritime project with due sensational headlines.

First Telegram. Not until April 30, 1851, was the first telegram sent from St. John to John Wilson. Curiously reads his answer from St. Andrews: "Being the first subscriber to the Electric Telegraph Company, I am honored by the first communication from your city announcing the great and wonderful work God has made known to man by giving us the control of the lightnings."

The Church. Neither steamboat, newspaper, nor telegram could make Campobello aught but a narrow confine for the social and political ambition of the Admiral. An exile because of poverty that compelled him to accept the royal gift, he felt that he must devote himself to controversial discussion and the erection of a new Episcopal church. Before this day the people had been Baptists; personal loyalty anglicized the religion of all those around Welch Pool.

Wilson's Baptists. The people at Wilson's, however, never abandoned their Baptist tenets, which they brought with them from the neighboring islands as they settled around Head Harbor. Those along the North Road rowed over to the larger settlement for baptisms and Sunday services, which were first held in the school-house, for the church itself was not built until some thirty-eight years ago.

North Road Baptists. At last the North Road residents had their own church, to which they were devotedly attached. The land for it cost forty dollars in gold paid down to Captain Robinson, as the proceeds of the efforts of sewing-circles and ladies' teas. The great Saxby gale of some twenty-five years ago blew it down.

Two years after it was rebuilt for $447, and finally finished ten years ago. The devoted Episcopalians at Welch Pool have made no greater sacrifices for their church than did the little band of zealous North Road Baptists. Though their regular ministers have been few, their irregular preaching and their prayer meetings have been constant.

Still it was but natural that, as the boys of the Baptist islands married the girls of St. George and other New Brunswick towns where the Church of England was the prescribed form of faith, Episcopalianism spread itself, not only among the islands in Passamaquoddy Bay, but at Campobello.

Church Corporation. Soon after Admiral Owen had become resident magistrate and commissioner for solemnizing marriages, to which the witnesses as well as the bridal couple signed their names, he signalized his authority by giving for three years certain wild lands as commons for cattle to those who should belong to the "Church Episcopal Congregation," when formed. The lease was duly signed by himself and by John Farmer, in trust for the people. Such privilege, even if actuated by worldly motives, proved of sacred benefit, for measures were immediately taken to form a Church Association and corporation, with the proviso that such persons as had decided objections to profess themselves members of the church could by no means become a part of such corporation. The Admiral's cattle ranged free in the commons, but on all other licensed and marked cattle were paid the fees which accrued to the benefit of religion, and large must have been the income thereof.

The regularly ordained preacher was sent from St. Andrews but four or five times a year. On all other appointed days the Admiral read his beloved service, even till 1842, when a resident missionary came to live on the Island. Thirteen years after, in 1855, the church and burial ground were consecrated by the bishop of the diocese. Most solemn and tender must have been those first rites, when confirmation was administered to three persons, and holy communion to forty others, in that little building surrounded by the dark balsamic firs, looking with its cross over the waters toward the New England steeples.

English friends sent money to the church, and the Owen family gave memorial offerings. The reredos, with its silver cross, was a memorial to Captain John Robinson, the grandson of the Admiral. The block of stone from which the font was carved was taken from the Church of the Knights Templar at Malta, and carried to Florence by the Admiral's son-in-law to be wrought into graceful form, and then was borne across the ocean to this tiny, much loved church. The chancel carpet, worked on canvas in cross-stitch; the altar vestments; the stoles; the chalice veils, green, white, crimson, purple, each bearing the symbol of the cross in varied stitch and design, — were all wrought by the delicate fair hands of the Admiral's daughter, and her children, and their friends, as an offering of self-consecration and of devotion to the building up of a higher life among the Islanders. These, too, brought their gifts, and replaced with chandeliers the wax candles which had been set in holes in the book-rests; and, when the sea called away the men, an old lady, rich in humility and good works, rang the bell for the weekly services.

Bishop Medley. Interwoven with the personal life of this church was the affection with which it was regarded by "The Most Eminent John Medley, D. D., Anglican Bishop of Fredericton, N. B., and Metropolitan of Canada, who died in 1892, at the advanced age of eighty-eight years. It was in this church that he married his second wife, who was a friend of Lady Owen's. He seldom failed to visit the Island every year or two, and was the trusted confidant of each man, woman, or child, who knew him, for his simplicity of life accorded with Island habits, and the people comprehended his singleness of purpose, even if they did not always go to church. The names of Mr. and Mrs. Medley often occur in the parish records as visitors of the Parish School, with which they seem to have been regularly pleased.

The Deanery. The Parish of Campobello was and is under the jurisdiction of the Deanery of St. Andrews. At its meetings, which were for purposes of social visitation as well as for church discipline, the Admiral talked to the Deans if not with them. He knew the law better than many of them, and had an eye to business. Earnest and simple are the records of these gatherings, as of the one at St. Andrews in 1852, when some wished that "all articles necessary to ornament and fitting of places of worship should be admitted free of duty"; yet the movement failed of approval lest action on behalf of it might "appear like a move of the church for exclusive privilege."

Church Lands. A later resolve of the Deanery reads as follows: "Resolved, that whereas Romanists, Presbyterians, Methodists, and other Sectarists, are busy in successfully seeking from the Government tracts of land, to be surveyed for their respective denominations, to be settled by their co-religionists, that the Rural Dean communicate with the Lord Bishop, and ask his advice whether it may not be wise to seek like tracts of land for the settlement of church families as soon as possible, lest there be left no lands for the settlement of churchmen."

Special Prayer. When the Deanery met at Campobello it was resolved that, "Owing to the special calling of the Inhabitants of the County, that the Bishop draw up a form of Prayer for public service for those so exposed, to be used at the discretion of the clergy."

In 1863, the Deans approved of employing a "Book hawker in the dissemination of Church books and tracts in the Province." "The prevailing sins of our time, especially those by which we are more immediately surrounded," was as favorite a topic of discussion in those days of Deanery meetings as it is now.

The Admiral's Stock Company. Among other documents belonging to the period of the Admiral's active life on the Island is a pamphlet printed in London in 1839, entitled "The Campobello Mill and Manufacturing Company in New Brunswick, British North America."

This Company was incorporated June 1, 1839, with a capital of $400,000 in two thousand shares at $200 each; interest at 6 per cent. was guaranteed on all sums actually paid on the shares, secured on the fixed property on the Islands and responsibility of the Company. The President was William Fitz-William Owen. There were also six Directors, who were all in official life, with the exception of "John Burnett, Esq., of Campobello, Merchant." The property, says the pamphlet, "is valued at \$100,000, and offers available means of employing five times the capital." The returns in four or five years would probably be twenty-five per cent, on the capital. The situation of the Island "is extremely commodious for commerce with Great Britain, the West Indies, and the United States." An early prospectus of the Company's extols the situation, because, by order of His Majesty in Council, Campobello was constituted a free Warehousing Port. Jacob Allan, Deputy Surveyor and Commissioner of Crown Lands, "certifies that there is now standing a sufficient quantity of spruce and pine of the finest growth for saw logs to keep four double saw-mills going for the space of forty years; that is, perpetually.... The fisheries on the coasts of the Island were let this year by the Company for near £400, and fish were taken on the coasts to the amount of £3,000." It is also "stated that there is a large quantity of ore about Liberty Point." The Company was incorporated "for the purposes of erecting, using, and employing all descriptions of mills, mill-dams, fulling and carding machinery, and will have a decided advantage over any other spot in British America." "The population would thus grow rapidly, and the Company, having the property of the whole coast, must become the medium of all exchanges with all the population, which now amounts to six hundred only."

Alas, the Admiral's dreams have never been realized. The saw-mills which were built long ago fell into decay. The ores, if there are any, are still unexplored; agriculture does not flourish; the fisheries have decreased, herring are scarce; and the various changes in the imposition of duties have perplexed and thwarted the business activity of the Islanders.

Admiral's Second Marriage. Year after year the Admiral saw his hopes deferred. Lady Owen had died. His daughter, Mrs. Robinson Owen, and her children, still lived in the Island home, helping, teaching, guiding all around them with kindliness and wisdom. But the Admiral spent most of the last five years of his life at St. John, for he married a Mrs. Nicholson of that city, whose maiden name was Vennell.

His Burial. His strange, pioneer, semi-royal, administrative career ended in 1857. The boat that bore him back from St. John for the last time to his hermitage ran aground; for the great falling tides bade him wait, even in the pomp of death, until it was their hour to bear him aloft on his oft-trod pier. Men, women, and children, seized lantern, candle, or torch, and carried their hermit lord over the rough stones and the narrow ways to the cemetery, where they buried him at eventide, amid the waving trees and with the sound of falling tears.

His memory nestles in the hearts of the children who play around the weirs, and who have learned from their grandsires the tales of his jokes, his oddities, and his kindnesses. His children and his grandchildren stayed in the primitive ancestral home till 1881, when the Island was sold to an American syndicate. As long as any of the Owen family lived there they were beneficent rulers of the people, and maintained a courtly standard of manners and morals, the grace of which lingers among the Islanders.

The Cannons again. Tradition and fact still invest the Owen name with tenderness and homage, as was shown on July 10, 1890, when the great-grandson of the Admiral revisited Campobello. Never has the old cannon belched forth its volume of sound more loudly than it did for Archibald Cochrane, who, as a boy, had often sat astride of it. A "middy" on board Her Majesty's flagship *Bellerophon*, he came back to his ancestral estates, accompanied by Bishop Medley. The boys' sunny blue eyes and gentle smile recalled his mother's beauty to the old Islanders. The Dominion Hag and the English flag waved from every ship in port and from the neighboring houses, to welcome him back. As the steamer came in sight, the aged cannon, mounted on four huge logs of wood, gave forth its welcome. Each time the cotton had to be rammed down, and the cannon had to be propped up. Each time the match and the lighted paper were protected by a board held across the breech at arm's length; but the brass piece did its duty, and the people called "well done" to it, as if it had been a resuscitated grandsire. The steamer answered whistle for cannon blast, and the children's laugh was echoed back across the water.

It was dead low tide—and the tide falls twenty feet—when the venerable bishop came up the long flight of steps, slippery and damp with seaweed. Guarded on each side and before and behind, with umbrella in his hand for his walking-stick, the metropolitan of eighty-four years accepted the unneeded protection which Church of England reverence dictated.

The Great-Grandson. But as the boy ran quickly up the same steps, there was not a man who did not rush forward to greet him. The band played, while the women crept out from among the piles of lumber and waited for recognition. It came as the boy was led from one to another, bowing low in his shy, frank manner, cap in hand, to the women and girls, who had known him as a child, and shaking hands heartily with all the men, young and old. Away off stood two old ladies, who blessed the morn which had brought back their young master. Up to them he went with pretty timidity, and then, boy-like, hurried off to look at the cannon. He put his finger on it with a loving touch and a lingering smile, which to the older ones who saw it told of hidden emotion, which, perhaps, he himself scarcely recognized.

Silence fell as the Metropolitan rose from the chair where he had been resting and thanked the people for their greeting to the boy, because of his grandparents. The midshipman's eyes shone as they fell on the faces, lighted up as they had not been for years, to see that the fair, five-year old boy who had left them had grown into the straight-limbed, graceful, manly, modest youth, whose greeting was as unaffectedly frank as their own. After a while midshipman and bishop stole silently away up to the graves of the old Admiral and his wife, of the captain grandfather, and the cousin, all of whom had been naval heroes.

The Old Home. On to the Owen house went the boy and found his old haunts,—first, the nursery, then his mother's room, and next his grandmother's; out among the pines to the places where he had played, on to the sun-dial and the quarter-deck. All were revisited, with none of the sadness which comes in middle life, but with the sure joy of a child who has found again his own. He clicked the uncocked pistols of the Admiral, and took up the battered, three-cornered hat.

In the afternoon a game of baseball was played in his honor; and never did his great-grandfather watch more eagerly for victory over the pirates than did this descendant watch that the game might be won by the Campobello boys. At evening, in the little English Church, where the bishop blessed the people and told of Lady Owen's deeds of mercy, the boy bent his head over the narrow bookrest, and after the service was over he again shook hands with those who had so easily and quickly become his friends.

The next day the people gathered again at the wharf. The midshipman was a new old friend by this time. Once more the brass-piece sounded farewell as he crossed the bay. It had been the playmate of his boyhood, his imaginary navy, his cavalry horse, his personal friend. By its side he had never wanted to rest on chairs or sofas. Once more he turned to look at it as he went down the steps to the water's edge, and waved adieu to those who loved him for his mother's sake, with a fondness and pride and sense of personal ownership unknown in "the States," where ancestry counts for but little.

The old cannon still stands upright in Mr. Batson's store. No one would ever steal it again. No one can ever buy it away. From father to child it will descend, to tell of the English-American feudalism of a hundred years ago, and of the happy, bright boy, who found his father's house turned into a modern hotel.

The wonderful loveliness of Campobello can never be taken from it by any possessor. It is a beauty partly its own, and partly borrowed from the soft rounded headlands, the toy-like islands, the vanishing rivers, and the far reaches up the bay, which make the opposite shore. Busy shining Eastport, with its New England steeples, spreads itself gently in a long line down to the water's edge.

The Sunsets. At evening the sunset sends its glory over the waters and the land, blending all into the wondrous charm of changing, glowing color. The sunsets of the Island have been likened to those of Italian skies and Swiss lakes. They need no comparison. They make their hours those of exceeding beauty and reverent silence.

Treat Island. Treat Island is one of the places which enhance the enjoyment of Campobello. It lies between Lubec and Eastport. Its first owner was Colonel John Allan, who gave it the name of Dudley Island, in recognition of his friend, Paul Dudley Sargent, a descendant of the Earl of Leicester. As Colonel Allan's revolutionary sentiments compelled him to leave Nova Scotia, his American patriotism eventually led to his appointment of Superintendent of the Indians. He thus became involved in perplexities and hairbreadth escapes. At the end of the war he went into business on Dudley Island, and counted among his guests Albert Gallatin. Allan was buried on the island in 1805. In 1860 two hundred of his descendants gathered there, and dedicated to his memory the marble column which the antiquarian and the picnic lover alike visit. After a while the island began to be known as "Treat's," for a gentleman of that name had bought it, and carried on there a large fish-curing business. He was also the successful pioneer of the canning industry. But with the scarcity of herring and multiplicity of duties, the weirs became disjointed and the houses dilapidated. Alas! now the land is hired for pasturage, and excellent thereof is the milk.

Benedict Arnold. Among Allan's customers when he lived on the island was Benedick Arnold; for Allan spelt the name with a *k*, as his account book shows. Arnold at that time, though in business at St. John, N.B., was living for a short time in Campobello, at Snug Cove. In the Centennial year this account book was exhibited at Dennysville, as one of its curiosities. In 1786 Arnold bought a new vessel, which he called the "Lord Sheffield," and made trading voyages in her along the coast and to the West Indies. Once, while cruising in Passamaquoddy Bay, he invited Colonel Crane to dine with him on board his vessel. But the Colonel, who was a revolutionary veteran, stamping his foot, wounded at the siege of New York, furiously replied, "Before I would dine with that traitor I would run my sword through his body." Arnold went to England in 1787, where he insured his St. John store and stock for £6,000. The next year he came back; a fire consumed all, and Arnold collected the insurance. Two years later Arnold's partner accused him of setting fire to the store. Arnold sued for slander, and claimed £5,000 damages. The jury awarded twenty shillings! When he left St. John his house was sold at public auction. "A quantity of household furniture," reads the advertisement: "excellent feather beds: mahogany four-post bedsteads, with furniture; a set of elegant Cabriole chairs covered with blue damask; sofas and curtains to match; an elegant set of Wedgewood Gilt Ware; two Tea-Table sets of Nankeen china; Terrestrial Globe; a double Wheel Jack; a lady's elegant Saddle and Bridle, etc." Yet whoever now owns them must be glad that they are not family heirlooms. Auction sales are more honorable for some china.

Smuggling. Whether Arnold was attracted to the Passamaquoddy region by its opportunities for smuggling can never be known. But certain is it that the embargo law of 1807 had put a stop to foreign trade, and in 1808 destroyed the coasting trade. Before then it had been easy to carry breadstuffs and provisions across the line. Thousands of barrels thus reached Eastport; and many thousands were brought to Campobello and Indian Island, at one dollar a barrel. Smuggling began, or, if it did not then begin, it increased. Sudden wealth and bad habits kept pace with each other. At first the price for smuggling was twelve and one-half cents a barrel, which quickly rose to three dollars a barrel. One man is said to have earned forty-seven dollars in twenty-four hours. Fogs helped,—"that's why they were made".

In the war of 1812, Indian Island and Campobello were very busy in shipping English goods and wares from the large colonial ports. Neutral voyages were constantly made. American vessels had a Swedish registrar, and went from Sweden to Eastport in three or four hours. Silk, wool, cotton, metals, were thus carried up the bays and streams, and shipped in wagons to the Penobscot, then to Portland, Boston, etc.

Provincial trade was peculiar. British vessels, laden with gypsum and grindstones, because they came from ports not open to American vessels, sailed to the frontier out on the lines, and transferred their cargo to American vessels waiting there. Slaves from Norfolk, Virginia, were sent to some neutral island, from there transported to an English ship again out on the lines, and then carried to the West

Indies.

Rice Island. One of the islands which was cognizant of some of the smuggling was Tuttle's, now called Rice Island, after Solomon Rice, who kept store there. It is a little round spot of beauty in the chain of islands bridged by fallen weirs, between Lubec and Eastport.

Lubec. Lubec itself owes its existence to the attempt of five citizens of Eastport to avoid the payment of duty bonds to the British. Lubec Point was then only a forest. Though by 1818 it had become a rival of Eastport, it is now but a small town. Yet it is more picturesquely situated than almost any other town in New England. Its single steeple and its flagstaff dominate the steep hill down which run two grassy streets to the water's edge, where stretch out into the Narrows the piers, which change their aspect with each rising and falling tide. When the fog sets in over the bay, the last point it hides is Lubec steeple. When it lifts, it leaves its gay flower gardens damp with a moisture that brightens each tiny petal. From the top of Mulholland's Hill, on Campobello, Lubec looks like some quaint foreign spot, with streaks of American activity across it.

Out beyond the town is Quoddy Lighthouse, built about 1809. Near it is the Life Saving Station. On the left of the hill are the low marshes off Lubec, and beyond them the long purple line of Grand Manan.

There is no more varied excursion than to row over to Lubec, and from there to drive through woods and over sandy roads to the lighthouse. Then drive back and along the upper shore to North Lubec, where the Young Men's Christian Associations have bought land and erected a hotel, with the privileges of fair accommodations and the enthusiasm of camp-meetings. At sunset take the Lubec Ferry to Campobello. There is so much to see in each place, and so many hills for the horse to walk up, that it is better to take two separate days for these drives.

Eastport. Another favorite pastime with the summer visitor is to row across to Eastport. It is the great shopping place, not only of Campobello, but of its own county. Most excellent and tasteful are its shops, whose proprietors have a courtesy of manner which city merchants might well emulate. The drives from Eastport are pleasant, each one different from the other. Go along the water up to Pleasant Point, where a few Indians live under the care of the kindly sisters of the Catholic Church, and where Rev. John Cheverus once visited, or over to Pembroke with its mills, and up and down long hills.

Meddy Bemps. Best of all is it to forsake the viands of the hotels, drive up to Meddy Bemps, and camp there for two or three days; catch what early fish you can, bass and pickerel; eat as big and as sweet blueberries as ever grow; pull up the water lilies by their long stems; buy rag mats; and enjoy the quiet and beauty of the lake and its shores.

The North Road. On Campobello itself the most lonesome and picturesque drive is that along the North Road, over stony and narrow ways, up rough hills, and by beaches which seem close to the houses. The view framed by the New Brunswick hills is ever changing, while the St. Croix River extends off into an unrimmed distance. From Head Harbor, lines of fishing boats, brilliant with the red flannel shirts of the men, stretch out into the bay. Eastport seems near and far. Part of the North Road is gay with gardens, for dearly do the Islanders love their dahlias, their princely flowers, and all the lesser floral dignitaries. Here stands the Baptist Church, against which the lambs crouch as if in sacrificial symbol. Far beyond it is Mallock's Beach, sentinelled by high cliffs, reverenced for generations as the baptismal beach. Then come the desolate, low peaks of bare, purple rock, which shut out all but gloom, when suddenly appear the bright, laughing waters of Havre de Lutre—Harbor of the Otter—and its opposite wooded shores, leading to Head Harbor. Let your horse find his own way homeward, and climb home yourself along the shores of Havre de Lutre, which will bring you out at the head of the harbor, near where William Owen first settled.

Head Harbor. The longest drive on the Island is to Head Harbor,—the Queen's Highway, as it is called,—past Cold Spring, Cranberry and Bunker Hills. Climb both, and you will never forget the view. Drive on past Conroy's Bridge, the schoolhouses, the church, Wilson's settlement (where do not fail to buy sticks of checkerberry candy), up and down the hills to Head Harbor River (where, report says, the Admiral once built a brig), to Head Harbor Beach, and there picnic. Then, refreshed by a lunch, which tastes better in the open air than indoors, walk over to the Fog Horn House, and, if the tide is right, go down a rocky hill, across a rocky ford, up a short iron ladder and on to Head Harbor Lighthouse. Never start on any excursion at Campobello until you have adjusted your hours to the tides, or else your plans will fail.

Mill Cove. This waiting upon the tide is of special importance at Mill Cove, the road to which branches off from Head Harbor road. There is no place on the Island equal to this for surprises. When the fog is "in" half of it is non-existent, as it were. At high tide you see an island which you cannot reach by carriage. At low tide you urge your horse up a short, pebbly beach, down into the water, and up on to an island. By permission of its occupant, you drive through his land out into a broad green field, with the Bay of Fundy fronting you, and the Wolves looking hopelessly lonely. Give a whole day to the weird and sunny beauty of the cove and its nooks.

Nancy Head. Between Mill and Schooner Coves are the White Rocks and Nancy Head, so called from a ship that was wrecked there.

Schooner Cove. Schooner Cove is another surprise, but a single one. After you have reached it, put on your rubbers and take the mile walk to the left along the cliffs. Ten years ago it was the most solemn trail that you could follow. Now, as civilization has come nearer, and sunlight has penetrated it, the grey moss hangs less heavily from the close branches, leafless even in summer, while the water dashes up over the rocks on the other side of the narrow path. On the right of the cove go with care, and at your peril, over the headlands, along the coves, and in through the almost untrodden forest to Herring Cove.

Here is the longest beach in Campobello, with curiously tinted and marked pebbles. It is but a mile through the woods, starting from the Tyn-Y-Coed, and is the favorite walk and drive of all those who like smooth and shady roads and an air laden with "spicy fragrance." On the left is Eastern Head, never to be forgotten as a place of exploration, with wonderful views from its points and down its ravines.

Herring Cove. A unique pleasure, which, though obtained by driving, cannot properly be counted among the drives, is the visit at night to Herring Cove, to see the men "driving the herring." Each wherry has a ball of cotton wool, or a roll of bark, on a stick saturated with kerosene, or else it is put into an iron cradle fastened to an iron pole. As the cotton or bark burns, the moving boats look like a fitful procession of lights. The brightness attracts the herring, and, as one man rows, while another "drives," the nets are hauled up full of wriggling, shining fish.

Lake Glen Severn, so called after the Owen place in Wales, is separated by a short bridge from the high beach before it slopes down to the water.

Meadow Brook Cove. Beyond Herring Cove is Meadow Brook Cove, an ideal place for the scene of a summer idyl. Into it runs a tiny brook which starts somewhere near the head of Havre de Lutre, marking the division which once took place in the Island, according to geologists. The ruins of a stone wall which runs along the brook are no longer supposed to have been built by the Northmen, for the Admiral erected it as part of his scheme in draining the meadow.

Branching off from the Herring Cove Road is the Fitz-William road, where many lots have been sold, and also the road to Raccoon Beach. This drive is along another wonderful tangle of forest skirted by beaches. It leads to Liberty Point, the cable line from Welsh Pool to Grand Manan passing by it, on to Skillet Cove, where there is a split rock, on again to Owen Head, desolate and vengeful in its height, down to Chalybeate Spring,—a fortune for the future,—across beaches too rough for a single team with four people, to Cranberry Point, and back to where you started. At Deep Cove, near the Point, is a rock bearing pronounced glacial marks. Take the drive at low tide, and feel its gloom, with the fog drifting across your face. Take it at high tide, on a sunny morning, and feel its cheerfulness.

Once more drive down to the Narrows, past the cottages; stop at Friar's Head, whose Indian name was *Skedapsis*, the Stone Manikin. Go to the pagoda-like structure on top of the hill, climb down its side, and at low tide go walk between the Friar and the hill; then at high tide wonder how you ever did it. Retrace your steps. Go along the road, past Snug Cove and the schoolhouse, till you come to the Narrows, where runs the swift current which only the experienced boatman can cross in his flat-bottomed boat, that carries alike the passenger or his horse, or brings over from Lubec the funeral hearse.

Yet these are not all the drives. Subdivisions of them lead you into marshes, plains, and woods, though they are preferable as bridle paths or walks. They began as cow-paths, and may end as country roads. Adventures can still be sought over dangerous cliffs. It is more than easy to get lost in the woods. Still, no matter where you go, you cannot help coming out somewhere near water and a fisherman's hut; for Campobello,—in Indian dialect *Ebauhuit*, signifying by or near the mainland,—having an area of twenty square miles, and a circumference of twenty-five miles, is ten miles long and two to three miles wide. Remember in all these drives to turn to the left, and when you walk not to be afraid of cows.

Perhaps it is the water excursions which render Campobello most famous. Among these is the sail to St. Andrews, which offers modern Wedgewood ware for sale, and where is the far-famed Algonquin Hotel and Cobscook Mountain. The West Isles and Le Tete Canal make another pleasant sail. To go around the Island on a calm day is delightful. Very exquisite in its limited beauty is the sail up St. George's River, the trees on either side arching their branches over the little steamer. St. George's Falls and the stone quarry should also be visited on landing at the pier.

Johnson's Bay. For a short outing, row across Friar's Bay to Johnson's Bay; climb the little hill to the pleasant, neat, and hospitable farm-house; go through a grove to the wooden look-out, and clamber upwards. For wondrous beauty of beach and land-locked bay, of great headlands and brown hay-cocks, of the mystery of nature's secretiveness in South Bay, the view is unsurpassed.

South Bay. Then, inspired by its loveliness, come home to the hotel, engage Tomar and his canoes, paddle across the wide bay, and in and out of the islands and crannies of South Bay, the happiest, sunniest, cosiest bay on the Maine coast. Go through the canal at high tide; paddle everywhere around till the tide turns, and you can pass back through this narrow and again water-filled canal into Friar's Bay, the cottages at Campobello serving as guide in steering the homeward course.

The Tides. But truly there never is any guide among the tides and currents setting in from the different islands and headlands save that of correct knowledge of their ways. To lose an oar in these waters might mean drifting for hours; and then if the fog sets in! That fog, which is the basis of conversation on first acquaintance, the spoiler of picnics, and the promoter of a beauty of landscape so infinite and varied that one only wonders how any summer place can be without it.

Dennysville. Yet, if any one chances to feel that he is too much a part of the fog in a row-boat, take the little steamer to Dennysville. The ebb and flow along the coast in this region is so marked, that in going up the Denny River the pilot carefully guides the steamer through the whirlpools and maelstroms, which are dangerous only in winter. The river grows very narrow, till at its source it seems to be set in meadow lands, along which one wanders, through the quiet village roads,—for the town is fifty miles from any railroad,—trying to comprehend why anybody should forsake a spot so soothing to the spirit and so simple in its loveliness for the confusion of city life.

Grand Manan. Of all the water excursions that to Grand Manan is by far the most rich in reward. The best way is to take the steamer Flushing, which runs three times a week from Campobello to Grand Manan, and spend two nights and one day there,—longer, if you wish. There is little fear of sea-sickness on board the big steamer. The extraordinary cliffs and the sixteen-mile drive to Southern Head are scenes never to be forgotten, but which beggar words to describe. The sternness of nature stands here revealed, and the moans of the sea-gulls tell of even their need of sympathy.

The Friar. Beside these cliffs the noted one of the Friar at Campobello seems comparatively short; yet it is the prominent rock of the Island as one approaches it, and its importance is increased by the legendary lore that has gathered around it. Mr. Charles G. Leland tells the story in this wise:—

"Once there was a young Indian who had married a wife of great beauty, and they were attached to each other by a wonderful love. They lived together on the headland which rises so boldly and beautifully above the so-called Friar. Unfortunately her parents lived with the young married couple, and acted as though they were still entitled to all control over her. One summer the elder couple wished to go up the St. John River, while the young man was determined to remain on Passamaquoddy Bay. Then the parents bade the daughter to come with them, happen what might. She wished to obey her husband, yet greatly feared her father, and was in dire distress. Now the young man grew desperate. He foresaw that he must either yield to the parents—which all his Indian stubbornness and sense of dignity forbade—or else lose his wife. Now, he was *m'teūlin*, and, thinking that magic could aid him, did all he could to increase his supernatural power. Then, feeling himself strong, he said to his wife one morning, 'Sit here until I return.' She said, 'I will,' and obeyed. But no sooner was she seated than the *m'teūlin* spell began to work, and she, still as death, soon hardened into stone. Going to the point of land directly opposite, over the bay, the husband called his friends, with his father-in-law and mother-in-law, and told them that he was determined never to part from his wife nor to lose sight of her for an instant to the end of time, and yet withal they would never quit Passamaquoddy. On being asked sneeringly by his wife's father how he would effect this, he said: 'Look across the water. There sits your daughter, and she will never move. Here am I gazing on her. Farewell!' And as he spoke the hue of stone came over his face, and in a few minutes he was a rock. And there they stood for ages, until, some years ago, several fishermen, prompted by the spirit which moves the Anglo-Saxon everywhere to wantonly destroy, rolled the husband with great effort into the bay. As for the bride, she still exists as the Friar; although she has long been a favorite object for artillery practice by both English and American vandal captains, who have thus far, however, only succeeded in knocking off her head."

Tomar. Many an Indian legend of doubtful authority still clings to various points on the Island; yet only the Indians themselves are persistent and real. Each summer day they bring their baskets for sale. Tomar, at one time governor of his tribe, on a small salary with large work to do, is one of the few thoroughbred Indians who still live in this region. He is a man of integrity, skill, and gentleness. Each visitor is eager to gain his companionship and guidance in his canoe, as he paddles into nooks where one less experienced might hesitate to penetrate. Greater than his skill in paddling is Tomar's ingenuity in scraping pictures on birch bark symbolical of Indian life.

His Tribe. The Passamaquoddy Indians, or Openangoes, were a branch of the Etechemin nation, and apparently of comparatively recent origin. Their earliest village near Campobello was at Joe's Point, near St. Andrews. The majority of the remnants of the tribe are found at Pleasant Point, near Eastport, at Peter Dana's

Point, near Princeton, and at The Camps, on the border of Calais. Their language is fast dying out; but their traditions and customs have been carefully studied and collected largely by Mrs. W. Wallace Brown, of Calais, and also by Professor J. Walter Fewkes, who has taken down on the wax cylinders of the phonograph many of their songs and stories.

The following original poem by one of the tribe was written for a sale that was held on August, 1883, for the benefit of a new rectory on the Island, in which Miss Lucy Derby was interested, and through whose efforts the rectory was built, the Company giving the land.

AMWES-WINTO-WAGEN.

Amwézik 'klithwon ya skedabe zogel;
Skedap tatchuwi melan kekousé kiziolgweh.
Ulzee-ik 'lee madjhé goltook kizosook;
Tatchuuwi tewebn'm nenwel kthlee-tahazoo wagenen woolsum'kik.
Piyemee absegékook beskwaswesuk tchicook
Pèmee woolip p'setawkqu'm'see you wen.
P'skèdab tatchuwè oolazoo weeahl m'pseeoo-wenil.
Amwess ooktee-in aboozek;
Uppes kootee-in hedlègit;
Beskwas'wess lookquem hahze;
Nojeemeeko gèmit chooiwigeou:
Weejokègem wee you'h.
Piel John Gabriel kweezee-toon yoot lin to wagun.
Kee zee skee jin wih tun;
Whu-titli keezeetoon Ebawg'hwit,
Wè jee kissi tahzik wenoch chigwam.
N'paowlin kweezee Iglesmani tun.

THE SONG OF THE BEES.

The bees make honey for man;
Man should give something to God.
The trees lift their tops to the sun;
We should lift up our hearts to our father.
The smallest flower in the forest
Gives out a perfume for all.
Man should do good unto all men.
The bee has a tree (for a home);
The tree has a place to grow;
The flower has a stem;
The clergyman must have a house:
May this song help it.
Peter John Gabriel made this song.
He made it in Indian;
He made it in Campobello (the island by the shore),
To help to build the house.

[1]N'pow-o-lin (the scholar, or man learned in mysteries) put it into English.

The Fenians. Among the Islanders are many whom it is delightful to know. They are all interested in affairs of church, school, and state, and eager for the future commercial prosperity of the Island. Excitement in local politics often runs high, but only once—in 1886—has there been resort to arms. Then the Fenians were at Eastport and Lubec. From the latter place some came over to low water mark, but were driven back "by the shine of the rifles"; for Captain Luke Byron, with one hundred and fifty Islanders, duly equipped, was stationed at the Narrows, Havre de Lutre, and Wilson's Beach. Though the Fenians were at Eastport but little more than a month, the Campobello committee of safety remained on guard three months. But when an English man-of-war came into the harbor, the Fenians, to avoid capture, sank their own vessel off the Narrows, beyond the lighthouse, and escaped themselves towards Machias.

Climate. The summer climate of Campobello is cool and delightful, the thermometer ranging between fifty-five and seventy-five degrees; so one can be outdoors all day long without becoming oppressed by the heat. The extensive forests of balsamic firs seem to affect the atmosphere, soothing and invigorating the visitor by day, and inviting sleep by night.

Water. The greater part of the Island is fertile. The common field and garden plants and vegetables grow abundantly, while the deep layer of drift gravel affords excellent well water at almost all points. The water supply for the hotels and cottages is, however, brought in pipes from distant springs, and filters itself by passing through a natural reservoir of sand.

Soil. The soil consists of a light clayey loam. "The general surface of the Island is marked by the sharply curved contours characteristic of all glaciated regions, where the rocks are of unequal hardness covered over by a deep bed of soil composed of the drift waste. This soil consists of a light clayey loam of rather remarkable fertility."—says Professor Shaler. "The greater part of the trees are evergreen, belonging to two species of fir and two of spruce. Scattered among them are the common species of birch, poplar, the common red beech, and in open swampy places the alder," which spreads with amazing rapidity.

Flowers. Wild Roses, varying in color from the palest pink to an almost magenta red, cover whole fields with their frail beauty. In the grass and round the ledges about Friar's Head the Campanula droops its blue bell. The Blue Iris skirts the borders of Lake Glen Severn. The Field Daisy, Sea-side Buttercup, the Marsh Pea, the Fall Dandelion, and the Sheep Laurel, spread themselves over the pastures in processions of color. The Wood Oxalis, its white petals veined with pink, and the Linnæa or Twinflower, are found half concealed beneath the underbrush of the woods. Among the rarer flowers of the Island is the Alpine Cloud Berry, or Amber Colored Raspberry, found on the Alpine summits of the White Mountains and on the Northeast Coast, which is the same as the Norwegian species. The Corn Chamomile, a rare weed, and the Wild Chamomile, both of which are nat-

---

[1] Mr. Charles G. Leland.

uralized from Europe, are found here, but chiefly around Eastport. The aromatic Wintergreen is the real Checkerberry, in Maine called the Trory Plum. The lovely Eyebright is found only along the coast of Maine and Canada; its Alpine form is rare. There are many varieties of Orchids, Asters, and Goldenrod, of Primroses, Honeysuckle, Heath, and of Lilies, from the Trillium or Trinity Flower to the two-leaved Solomon's Seal.

The wild strawberry in July, and the blueberries and raspberries in August, and the small cranberry in September, give occupation to the children, whose prices for berries are variable.

In the waters around the Island there "is a richer animal and vegetable life than is found along any other part of our shore."

Dispute about Names of Rivers. These waters have been the subject of constant litigation from early days. According to the oldest maps, the present St. Croix River was called Magaguadavic, and the Schoodic River, the Passamaquoddy; a name applied not alone to that River, but to the bays of Schoodick, St. Andrews, Cobscook, the waters from around Head Harbor (Campobello), to West Quoddy, etc., on account of the great number of pollock taken in these waters. The Magaguadavic received its present name of St. Croix from a cross erected there by the French, before there were any English settlers in its neighborhood. The dispute concerning the identity of these rivers, interesting as an historical matter, has not the political importance which attaches to the settlement of the boundary line between the American and English possessions.

Boundary Line. This line goes out "between Deer Island and Campobello, so as to give the United States equal access through the main channel to the sea, and then remands Campobello into British territory," for, by the treaty of 1783, all islands heretofore within the jurisdiction of Nova Scotia were to remain British territory.

The Owen. All this now is a matter of almost antiquarian concern, the present interest centering in the development of the Island as a summer resort. In 1881 it was purchased of the Owen heirs by a few New York and Boston gentlemen, who organized the Campobello Land Company. The Owen was at once built upon the site of Admiral Owen's private domain. Part of this dwelling house was moved across the gravelled walk to serve as an office for the Company and in it were placed the Owen relics. The rest of the house was left unaltered, the lower rooms serving as hotel offices and the upper ones as chambers. The following year a larger dining room for the hotel was constructed, William G. Preston being employed as architect of the whole structure.

Tyn-Y-Coed. In 1882 the Tyn-Y-Coed was opened, in 1883 the Tyn-Y-Maes, both erected under the supervision of Cummings and Sears, of Boston.

Cottages. The first cottages which were finished in 1884 were those of James Roosvelt, Esq., of New York, and Samuel Wells, Esq., of Boston. Dr. Russell Sturgis, of Boston, Travers Cochran, Esq., of Philadelphia, Alexander Porter, Esq., and Gorham Hubbard, Esq., of Boston, Alfred Pell, Esq., of New York, have each successively built summer residences on the Island.

In 1892 The Owen and its adjacent land and Man-of-War Neck were sold to some Boston gentlemen, who intend to manage the Owen as a summer hotel.

Each year the place becomes better known, but those who early made it their summer home have stamped upon it, it is hoped, that simplicity in manner of living which will prevent it from ever becoming either a place for picnics or a fashionable resort. It can never lose the picturesque beauty and the exhilarating climate which make it a most beautiful summer sojurn from May to November, for the autumn months are as glorious in clearness of atmosphere as the early summer months are lovely in their softness of verdure and coloring, while the sunsets always kindle the imagination into visions of the future.

LECTOR HOUSE LLP
E-MAIL: info@lectorhouse.com